Copyright notice

Copyright © *2021*, Marlon E. Plaatjies.

License to use e-book

(e)   use the e-book or any part of the e-book for a commercial purpose.

You must retain, and must not delete, obscure or remove, all copyright notices and other proprietary notices in the e-book.

The rights granted to you by this disclaimer are personal to you, and you must not permit any third party to exercise these rights.

If you breach this disclaimer, then the license set out above will be automatically terminated upon such breach (whether or not we notify you of termination).

Upon the termination of the license, you will promptly and irrevocably delete from your computer systems and other electronic devices any copies of the e-book in your possession or control, and will permanently destroy any paper or other copies of the e-book in your possession or control.

Digital rights management

You acknowledge that this e-book is protected by digital rights management technology, and that we may use this technology to enforce the terms of this disclaimer.

Pirate copies

If you have bought or received a copy of this e-book from any source other than us or *www.amazon.com* then that copy is a pirate copy. If this has happened to you, please let us know by email to *support@themlmfenix.com*.

You can buy a genuine copy of the e-book from *www.amazon.com*

No advice

The e-book contains information about The Mechanisms of Money and *Financial Planning*. The information is not advice and should not be treated as advice.

You must not rely on the information in the e-book as an alternative to financial advice from an appropriately qualified professional. If you have any specific questions about any such matter you should consult an appropriately qualified professional.

You should never delay seeking legal advice, disregard legal advice, or commence or discontinue any legal action because of information in the e-book.

Limited warranties

Whilst we endeavor to ensure that the information in the e-book is correct, we do not warrant or represent its completeness or accuracy.

We do not warrant or represent that the use of the e-book will lead to any particular outcome or result

To the maximum extent permitted by applicable law, we exclude all representations, warranties and conditions relating to this e-book and the use of this e-book.

Limitations and exclusions of liability

Nothing in this disclaimer will:

(a)   limit or exclude any liability for death or personal injury resulting from negligence;

(b)   limit or exclude any liability for fraud or fraudulent misrepresentation;

(c)   limit any liabilities in any way that is not permitted under applicable law;

(d)   exclude any liabilities that may not be excluded under applicable law; or

(e)   limit or exclude any mandatory rights that you have as a consumer under applicable law.

The limitations and exclusions of liability set out in this disclaimer:

(a)   are subject to the preceding provision; and

(b)   govern all liabilities arising under this disclaimer or relating to the subject matter of this disclaimer, including liabilities arising in contract, in tort (including negligence) and for breach of statutory duty, except to the extent expressly provided otherwise in this disclaimer.

We will not be liable to you in respect of any losses arising out of any event or events beyond our reasonable control.

We will not be liable to you in respect of any business losses, including (without limitation) loss of or damage to profits, income, revenue, use, production, anticipated savings, business, contracts, commercial opportunities or goodwill.

We will not be liable to you in respect of any loss or corruption of any data, database or software.

We will not be liable to you in respect of any special, indirect or consequential loss or damage.

Trade marks

*The **Mechanisms book series and Marlon E. Plaatjies Global**,* our logos and our other registered and unregistered trademarks are trademarks belonging to us; we give no permission for the use of these trademarks, and such use may constitute an infringement of our rights.

The third party registered and unregistered trademarks and service marks that feature in our e-book are the property of their respective owners and, unless stated otherwise in this disclaimer, we do not endorse and are not affiliated with any of the holders of any such rights and as such we cannot grant any license to exercise such rights.

Law and jurisdiction

This disclaimer shall be governed by and construed in accordance with South African law.

Any disputes relating to this disclaimer shall be subject to the exclusive jurisdiction of the courts of South Africa.

Page Left Blank Intentionally

This e-book is dedicated to the love of my life
My wife Verlene, the light of my universe,
And to the two greatest blessings in my life,
Leyshaen and Matthew, the oysters of my world
Who supported me throughout it all,
I truly love and appreciate you all.

Marlon E. Plaatjies

Page Left Blank Intentionally

TABLE OF CONTENTS

INTRODUCTION

Have you ever wondered how some people can create financial freedom for themselves and their families with seemingly zero effort?

Ever wondered how some people seem to live happy, fulfilling lives and have time freedom and live their best lives?

Have you ever asked yourself what it is that **they** do that you don't?

You are not alone…

I too spent nearly all my adult life wondering about this and always asked myself what it is that they do differently.

So, in an effort to understand this, I embarked on a journey to discover what the **SECRETS** were that the Financially Free of this world knew that was hidden from so many of us.

This led to me reading countless books, listen to tons of audiobooks, I've watched hours and hours of video seminars and I studied programs on **Wealth Creation Systems**.

I found that there were a few, *very **distinct**,* differences between myself and the people who have created **Financial Freedom** for themselves and when I started implementing everything I learned, **my life changed**!

In this E-Book, I will detail the **PRINCIPLES** that creates Financial Freedom. I will also provide you with a **Formula** that will help you create Financial Freedom for yourself and your family. *Sounds good?* Great!

This e-book serves as a guide that will give you better insights into the methods that create Financial Freedom.

It provides you with principles and strategies that will help you escape the "*Pit of Financial Despair*".

It is worth mentioning that the information in this book is NOT for everyone, however, those who are **serious** about taking control of their Finances will benefit greatly from its contents.

Let's begin by looking at a snapshot of some Factual Data and Statistics. As you read through the stats, run a mental checklist and see how many of these facts apply to you right now...

PART ONE
FACTS AND STATS

Before we dig into the more strategic and tactical stuff, let's have a look at the current situation in our country.

SA's Income and Earnings Stats:
- The current *minimum wage* in SA is **R21.69 per hour**
- Salaries in SA range from R7, 880 (minimum salary) to R139, 000 (maximum average is higher) per month
- The median (middle salary value) is around R29, 900 per month
- 50% (half of the population) earn less than R29, 900 per month
- The other 50% earn more than that
- The *average* worker gets paid around R22, 500 per month or +/- R270, 000 per annum

Now that we have an idea of what South Africans earn, let's take a look at some scarier facts and stats.

SA's Household Financial Stats:

➢ Most South Africans are "broke" by the *15th* of the month
➢ More alarmingly, **76%** of South Africans run out of money **before** month end
➢ **59%** of us borrow from friends and family every month
➢ **20%** make use of credit cards
➢ **9%** take out loans (this number does not include "mashonisa" loans)
➢ **76%** use the borrowed money for non-essentials like *Fast Food* and *Alcohol*

The 3 biggest expenses for SA households are:
1. Housing – A massive 41% is expensed on housing
2. Groceries – Accounts for 24% of our expenses
3. Transport – Takes up 10% of our monthly income

The top 3 expenses in SA households make up a massive **75% of our total income**, the other 25% of our income covers, school fees, servicing debt, supporting family/friends, health, clothing and security to name a few. There are many other variables that contribute to the financial status of SA households. I merely highlighted a few in order to point out the importance of understanding money and the mechanisms by which it operates.

From the statistics above, it is clear that we need **practical** and **viable solutions** to help us take control of our finances with a key aim and focus on **Financial Freedom**.

Let us look towards the future. Let's focus our energy on the solution and no longer on the problem or the current *"Status Quo"*.

"We must be the change we want to see" - *Mahatma Gandhi*

PART TWO
PRINCIPLES

Our journey towards Financial Freedom and stability must first be subjected to a few vital principles. Principles form the basis of this process and everything you do from this point onwards stems from the principles you will learn here.

The word principle is a word that is commonly used in our society, however, have you ever stopped to think about the actual meaning of the word? Yes? No? Uuuhh???
The word PRINCIPLE has its origins in both Old French and Latin. In the Old-French the word is "*Principe*" and it means "*origin or cause*" and in Latin the word is "*Principium'*" and it means "*beginning, first part or commencement*".

The definition of the word according to the Merriam-Webster dictionary is as follows:

"*a Comprehensive and fundamental law, doctrine or assumption*".

This means that a Principle is all-encompassing (Covers everything) and of core (Central) importance to *something*. In this case, your MONEY.

With that said, let's go through some of the principles for Financial Freedom.

Principles for Financial Freedom

We are about to look at the principles that creates financial freedom for you and your family. It will be an injustice on my part if I fail to mention the stupendous importance of understanding the psychological aspect of this whole process.

For a lot of us the notion that we will never be able to get out of debt or become financially free is a greater challenge than getting out of debt and becoming financially free. READ THAT AGAIN!

Our beliefs therefore, is the number one factor to conquer and overcome.

This guide, aims to, not only help you become financially free, but also to develop a mindset that believes it is possible and can be achieved.

In order to get Your Money Right, you first have to Get Your HEAD right!

Getting your head right takes discipline, determination and consistency. That being said, you don't have to take gigantic steps towards achieving financial freedom, you don't have to pull your hair out, NO! it starts with small, daily disciplines that eventually lead to successful weeks, months, years and ultimately, Financial Freedom. So,

RELAX! YOU'VE GOT THIS!

The Principles described here does not require you to live a life of frugality or to live below your means (although in some cases this will be necessary in the initial stages of the process).

The Formula is underpinned by one fundamental law, that can be described in three words:
- Consciousness
- Implementation
- Results

If these steps are followed as advised and if it is implemented on a continuous basis, Financial Freedom is Imminent.

Now for the principles…

PRINCIPLE #1 – The Plans of The Diligent (the meticulous)

"If you fail to plan, you're planning to fail" – Benjamin Franklin

This famous adage is used by so many of us so often, but in reality, it is practiced by very few.

Moreover, those who do plan never follow through with their plans or execute what is dictated by the plan.

What, then, is the reason for the lack of planning or the poor execution of our plans?

The answer is twofold, (1) Zero Commitment to create a plan, and (2) lack of Discipline in the Implementation of a plan.

Those who do not plan, fail in both areas. Those who do plan but do not see their plans through, fail in the implementation of such plans.

So, what can be done to change this?

Firstly, if you do not have a financial plan, you have to do the following:
1. Make a commitment to commit yourself to create a Financial Plan and then, commit to committing to your commitments. Simply stated, DO WHAT YOU SAID YOU WILL DO AND FOLLOW THROUGH, NO EXCUSES!
2. Begin right away to draft a Financial plan, DO NOT WAIT until you have the right pen or notebook or the right budget program or tool. Take a book, any book, and BEGIN RIGHT AWAY to write a plan.
3. Put your plan into action, get it to the testing phase so that you can understand where you need to improve and make adjustments.

Secondly, if you already have a Budget or Financial Plan, you have to do the following:
1. Look at your plan and ask yourself these questions
   - Is my financial plan sound?
   - Does it bring me peace or cause more anxiety?
   - What can I do to improve the plan?

- o How can I get more out of it?
- o What is the goal and purpose of my plan?

2. If you find any flaw in your current plan, begin at once to draft a second edition of the plan, this will require you to have an in depth look at your finances and to probe for possible areas of improvement

3. TAKE ACTION by putting your revised plan to work. Testing the plan in the real world is the only way you will be able to prove its soundness.

PRINCIPLE #2 – What You Don't Track, Creates Lack

"What gets measured, gets managed" – Peter Drucker

When I ask people if they know what they did with their money in the last 30 days, and if they can tell me exactly how they spent their hard earned "Randelas", the answer is a resounding NO!

Why? Because we don't have systems in place to measure how we spend our money, how much we spend, where the money goes, what happened to it and when it left our bank accounts or wallets.

Ever heard people say, "My salary vanished into thin air" or "There is more month at the end of my money" or "My money leaves my bank account as soon as it enters it".

These statements are all too common and some of us probably use them every single month (if you could see my face right now).

Yet, when you survey these individuals and their spending habits you find that it is not the **lack of money** that causes distress and anxiety in their lives but rather their extravagant and lavish **spending habits**.

These are the same people who have 2 credit cards, 3 clothing accounts, Bank Loans, owe 4 different mashonisa's, drives luxury cars or a VrrrPaaa, buys expensive liquor every weekend, purchases take-aways every day and COMPLAIN... that they don't have enough money (Shocked face).

I am not against any of these things and I firmly believe that every single hardworking South African deserve to have these things and much more. I am merely asserting that in a lot of cases money isn't the problem but rather the way we spend it and more importantly **the source from which these purchases are made**. I am also not implying that there aren't individuals and families who find themselves in real financial dilemmas.

It is for this very reason that I put together this guide, to help my fellow South Africans who are in Financial Ruin get out of it in the shortest, possible space of time.

Why is tracking your finances so important?

In my research I found that Tracking is a standard in nearly every field of expertise. In soccer, for example, every single activity is tracked and documented, they can tell you exactly how many goals a player scored, how many games he or she played over the span of their entire careers, and so many other facts and stats. I find this remarkable as they do this with sheer precision. I can name various other examples of how Tracking plays a pivotal role in the measurement and management of the success of sports stars, businesses and other areas of life; however, the point here is to help you understand the role tracking plays in everyday life, especially when it comes to your **money**.

Yet the average South African does not apply this crucial step to their financial planning. When I learned this, it blew my mind. My wife and I learned about Tracking when we read the New York Times Best Seller by Darren Hardy, *"The Compound Effect"*.

Tracking has become a key principle in the way we manage our money and it has changed our spending habits completely. It has provided us with insights about our finances that had previously eluded us. Like most of you, we also squandered our income and earnings on what we deemed to be important. This was a grave error on our part especially once we learned the *Mechanisms of Money*.

7 Simple Steps TO Track Your Spending

Step One: Decide on a Maximum Daily Spending (MDS) limit for both you and your partner.

Step Two: Review exactly how much money you have available to spend. This includes every single item you spend money on not just the essentials.

Step Three: Get a pocket-sized notebook and a pen and keep it with you at all times (If you and your partner have separate bank accounts then get one for each of you)

Step Four: Every time you take out your wallet or your debit/credit card, you take out your notebook as well. This is **EXTREMELY IMPORTANT**!

Step Five: Make a note of everything you spent during the course of the day and, **wherever possible**, obtain cash receipts or till slips.

Step Six: Keep the slips in the notebook in the order of the *date of purchase* i.e., Monday 28/06/2021, KFC R60 (Notebook entry) and the accompanying receipt.

Step Seven: At the end of each day, you reconcile (balance) the books. i.e., What is written in the notebook vs the receipts. The total amount in your notebook and the total of the of **all** the receipts of the day should be the exact same (In balance).

This exercise seems cumbersome at first but after a few short days you should be doing it effortlessly and enjoying the process.

It is worth mentioning that this process is aimed at helping YOU become Financially Free so, being dishonest or trying to cheat the system will be to your own detriment, NO ONE ELSE's.

PRINCIPLE #3 – Your Financial Plan Is A *Net Income* Activity

This principle, though obvious to most, still evades others. A lot of people still budget from their GROSS income (Salary before deductions) rather than their NET Income (Actual funds paid into your bank account). As an example: Suppose you earn R20 000 per month and your "take home salary" is R16 000. Your budget, should be drawn up based on your "take home salary", in other words, the R16 000 **NOT** your gross salary of R20 000.

The biggest reason for this is because most people plan their budgets before their money reflects in their bank accounts. That's erroneous to say the least. Now you might say, but Marlon, I know exactly how much money comes into my account every month and I know exactly how much my expenses will be. True as that may be, and, **THIS IS VERY IMPORTANT**, most budgets do not make provision for VARIABLE EXPENSES.

Your Financial Plan consists of Fixed Expenses (Expenses that does NOT change frequently) and Variable or Fluctuating Expenses (Expenses that changes frequently). **Most individuals budget their Fixed Expenses and just wing their Fluctuating Expenses**. This is where we mess up big time! It is the little **unaccounted-for** expenses here and there that leave us with "more month at the end of our money".

Here Is A Good Tip:

Let's say that your company pays R15 184 into your account every month without fail, rather than budgeting on the whole sum in your account, always round the total amount off the zero digits i.e., R15 184 to R15 000. If you get Paid R15 999 you still round it off to R15 000 and start your financial plan based on the rounded off amount. The additional funds will come in handy for banking charges or when you are in need of some extra cash.

PRINCIPLE #4 – Pay Yourself First

"Pay yourself first. Do something that your future-self will thank you for" – Itaba David

To **pay yourself first** simply means:

Before you **pay** your bills, before you buy groceries, before you do anything else, set aside a portion of your income **for yourself**.

When I first learned this rule, my mind was blown to smithereens. I couldn't grasp this concept and its meaning, I admit I was a wuss, LOL! When I finally investigated the matter, I learned that this is one of the ways the rich get richer.

Paying yourself first is the key to ensure that you always have money, or cash-flow. Most budgets or financial programs out there do not make provision for this at all. It is such a powerful principle and will instantly change the way you handle your finances.

The idea is to pay yourself at least 10% of your **gross nett salary**.

The goal is to **increase** your Cash-flow by increasing your income and keeping your expenses low.

PRINCIPLE #5 – Giving Is Receiving

"Giving is in alignment with your purpose" – Dr Wayne Dyer

This principle is not only a matter of values but also a matter of your purpose in life. There is a beautiful song that really captures the essence of Giving, it simply says:

"If you want more happy than your heart will hold
If you want to stand taller if the truth were told
Take whatever you have and give it away.

I'm not saying give everything you own away, or go and sell everything you've worked hard for and give the proceeds from the sale away, NO! that would be ridiculous!

The day I learned that Giving is the exact same thing as Receiving, everything changed for me and my family. My mother always said, "The hand that gives is more blessed than the hand that receives". And boy was she right!

All it requires is that you sacrifice a small portion of your earnings as a gift to give away freely, with an open heart and mind to benefit those in need. That's it! You decide, based on the values you hold most dear, which organization, charity or family (for that matter) you will bless every month.

When we started doing this, we donated a meagre R50 to a children's charity of our choice, now we donate 10% of our total monthly income to charities and causes we value. Try this and watch your **blessings** roll in!

PRINCIPLE #6 – Prepare for The Rainy Days

"Without rain there is no life" – Jerry Yang

The COVID-19 pandemic has been the single greatest economically destructive event in our lifetime. The impact of the virus has proven, beyond reasonable doubt, that governments, businesses and families are not prepared for a cataclysmic event of this magnitude.

Given the current economic stance of the world, it goes without saying that there is no better time than now to prepare for the "Rainy days". According to an article by the Business & Human Rights

Resources Centre on the 16th of July 2020, "Three million South Africans lost their jobs as a result of the covid-19 lockdown."

Of those families, how many were financially prepared to weather the impact of such a storm? Think about it… This is scary and heart-breaking.

We have to ensure that we make saving for a rainy day, a budgetary priority! It is non-negotiable. We have to do this for ourselves and our loved ones.

Once again, saving for a rainy day does not require that you sacrifice 100% of your income towards saving, nor does it require that you become credulous and prevent yourself from living. All it requires is that you dedicate a small portion of your salary towards a "Rainy Day" savings account.

There are great ways to do this, like the Tax-Free Savings Account or TFSA offered by banks and other institutions like Old Mutual. These accounts allow you to save your money (up to a certain amount) and earn an interest on it that is not subject to taxation. You can learn more about these types of accounts here: www.oldmutual.co.za

I personally love investing my savings into stocks through the Easy Equities platform, here you can start purchasing stocks from as little as R10 (at the time of this writing). There are various other vehicles for you to save your hard-earned money in. Check out Easy Equities here: www.easyequities.co.za

Disclaimer: Please ensure that you do your research and homework before you purchase stocks or invest in any company or cause. There are a lot of scams out there and you don't want to end up losing your money by not doing due diligence.

PRINCIPLE #7 – Emergencies Are Inevitable, Plan for It

There is a reason this principle follows Principle #6, the two go hand in hand like salt and pepper at restaurants. In this process the two are not much different in it that they both prepare you for a rainy day, however, the difference between them is that the one is more liquid (can be accessed at any time) and the other forms part of your investment strategy.

In essence the one will be tapped into before the other. So, when in need you will first tap into your Emergency Fund and once it has been exhausted (which will hopefully not happen), only then will you access your savings.

Therefore, in your Financial Plan, your emergency fund takes up a bigger portion of your income than the savings do (More on this in Part Three).

PRINCIPLE #8 – 50% Can Go A Long Way, If Done Correctly

This principle is truly the **crux** of this entire process. It is truly the place one needs to get to in order to start seeing the true power of financial-discipline.

The goal, ultimately, is to save **40%** of your income. This requires a lot of work and happens over time. Getting to this point however, is really a great achievement.

At first it seems impossible to believe or even fathom that one could live on only half of one's income, but I assure that it is not just possible but attainable within a space of 12 months or less.

A lot of budget programs make use of the 50/20/30 formula which states that 50% of your salary should cover your needs, 20% should go towards investing and the remaining 30% should cater for your wants.

I challenge this formula for a few reasons. Firstly, it does not cater for some of the more important things in life like, giving and instead focuses 30% of your income on dining out, entertainment and travel (nothing wrong with that) but you are in a financial rut that will require you to put a hold on such things until you can expense a great deal of your money on the niceties of life.

The other reason I challenge this formula is because it advises individuals to spend their hard-earned money on the niceties life has to offer, rather than advising them to build up assets that will generate passive income and the passive income (money you did not work for) in turn will pay for the niceties of life without having to fork out your "busting your ass income" on these things.

Grant Cardone says it best in a video in which he addresses the hip-hop and sports stars in the USA, he asserts, "Buy the BS, just don't buy it from your Busting Your Ass Income."

Learning to live on 50% of your income and covering all your expenses from this 50% is so powerful that once you experience it you will no longer want to structure your budget any other way. From this 50% you pay everything. Yes EVERYTHING!

The truth is, creditors are always willing to negotiate with you regarding your accounts, the problem is that we avoid creditors like the plague instead of being open and transparent about our financial status. That is why we find ourselves blocking calls from our creditors... AM I TALKING TO SOME OF YOU HERE? Come on now...

Sit down with or phone your creditors and negotiate a repayment plan for your debts, the credit managers at every creditor are more than willing to negotiate, provided that you commit to the new payment plan. So, ensure that once you've made an arrangement, you STICK to it. I cannot stress the importance of this more!

Build up a nest egg for yourself and be patient, this stuff takes time. There is no get rich quick scheme, no get rich quick magic wand that instantly gives you an abundance of riches overnight! Anyone who sells you this type of road-to-riches nonsense clearly does not understand the mechanisms and dynamics of wealth creation.

PRINCIPLE #9 – Robbing Peter to Pay Paul

The meaning of this principle is as follows:

"To take from one in order to give something owed to another"

We borrow money to pay our bills, we borrow money from one loan shark to pay the other loan shark, we borrow money from one bank to pay another. This ladies and gents, is the true meaning of Robbing Peter to Pay Paul.

At one point in my life my borrowing became so bad that I only paid interest payments to the loan sharks. That is a bad place to be. Is this the case for some of you? Or do you do this with your overdraft? Or is it a Credit Card addiction? It was all of the above for me once.

The other meaning of Robbing Peter to Pay Paul is this, Not paying Woollies so that you can pay Truworths and the next month you have to do the opposite, pay Truworths and rob Woollies. This is a formula for disaster as I'm sure you've come to realize.

As mentioned in the previous principle, instead of avoiding creditors, rather make it a priority to negotiate a lower repayment plan that is more affordable for you and that will ensure that your creditors are able to collect from you every single month.

Now there are various reasons for making sure that you stick to these arrangements once made, reasons such as, your credit score, credibility and trustworthiness. I remember when I ran into some trouble with the bond payments on my first property the bank made every effort to help me and my ex-wife. They allowed us to pay off the outstanding amount over a period of 3 years or so by just paying an additional R1000 on our bond. This is evidence that creditors aren't the enemy.

Making arrangements with creditors does not come without conditions, usually one of the conditions is that, if you miss one payment without consulting the creditor ahead of time, the arrangement will be revoked and you would be liable to pay the full amount or face legal action and blacklisting.

Put your Pride aside, do what is right, so that you can live a peaceful life while you are working towards Financial Freedom. It will pay off in the long run.

PART THREE
10/10/10/20/50

A Formula for Financial Freedom

"A budget lets you decide what is worth spending your money on" -
Unknown

The following formula is my **Personal Financial Plan Formula** that I used to get myself out of financial debt and to financial freedom.

I named it 3 tens, a twenty and a fifty as a catchphrase that will stick and help me better remember how to structure my finances.

The plan works on percentages i.e., 10%, 10%, 10%, 20% & 50% hence 3 tens, a twenty and a fifty (see what I did there)

Here's the breakdown of the plan:

1st Ten - Pay Yourself First, the first 10, this is the **first line** in your PFP, this comes before anything else, including tights. Yes, before anything! This is your wealth building funds.
Please note this money is not for personal or any other use except for Wealth Building.

2nd Ten – Tights/Donations/Charities/Giving, the next 10, for some people this is the first line in the budget and that is absolutely beautiful, however, I want you to think about this, if you don't give to yourself, how will you be able to justify and sustain giving to others? You can't give what you don't have. If you belong to a church community, you can most certainly donate money to that particular organization. For those who aren't spiritually affiliated with a church community the best place for you to do this is by supporting causes and charitable organizations that are close to your heart. I cannot **stress** the importance of giving enough. It is said that a giving heart is more blessed than a receiving hand, and I for one concur and subscribe to this notion. You should too!

3rd Ten - Savings, the last 10 goes towards savings, this is your **"Honey Jar"** savings account. Like the 1st 10, this money is not to be touched as this money goes towards long term goals like saving towards a holiday, down payment on a car, Christmas goods, gifts, school wear and so on.

The Twenty – Emergency Fund, this money is the money you put away **"In Case of Emergency"**. This is the fund you dig into in the event that something happens or something goes wrong like your car breaking down or the geyser bursting and you have to pay the nauseating excess, bleh!

The Fifty – Operating Money, Ah finally! The day you can learn to live off half of your salary is the day you start creating wealth for yourself and your loved ones. If you truly want to create financial freedom this is the place you want to get to financially, this is freedom, this is self-discipline, this is true power! It will take some work and a lot of self-control, but the rewards are massive and you will thank yourself in a year or two's time. The Fifty covers any and all other expenses you have on a monthly, weekly and daily basis.

This is how I would structure your PFP and the FP for your business. You want to get to a place where you save and **invest** about **40% (forty percentage)** of your monthly income.

If you start to apply this principle and implement these strategies, your finances will be restored to the "Green Zone" in no time.

With patient persistence, pig-headed discipline, determination and commitment, by practicing self-discipline and self-control you too can restore your money matters to order in a few short months and years and enjoy the benefits of Financial Freedom.

CONCLUSION

Money, though finite, has the ability to create the life you've always dreamed of. Money in and of itself does not have intrinsic value, the value of money is harnessed by the minds of men and women who make the effort to truly understand the mechanisms and dynamics of how it works.

There are various other resources that can teach you more in-depth strategies about how money works, how to use it, what the actual difference between assets and liabilities are and numerous other topics pertaining to finances. This guide focuses on Financial Freedom and Budgeting with the aim of helping you become Financially Free and live a life free of the burden of debt, stress and anxiety.

I owe my understanding of money and its inner workings whole heartedly to the book "Rich Dad, Poor Dad" by world renowned author, businessman and investor, Robert Kiyosaki. I suggest you

get this book and read it at least twice. It will change your life. Other
books that also had a great impact on my life are:
1.   Think and Grow Rich by Napoleon Hill
2.   Work the System by Sam Carpenter
3.   The Compound Effect by Darren Hardy
4.   The E-myth by Michael E. Gerber
5.   The Bible
And many other books that helped shape my mind and life.
If I could leave you with one thing, and if this is the only thing you
take from this guide, I would have done my part. It simply says:

*Your life is a result of all the choices you've made up to this point,
purchasing this guide is one of those choices. Make the most of the
time you have, live a life of discipline, honesty, live to love and
laugh, believe that great things can happen to you and for you and
expect these things to happen. Pour your life out for the benefit of
others and always, always trust in the Most-High. This my friend, is
the essence of living your best life.*

*Make Peace a priority and as far as possible, be kind to others, even
those who spitefully do you wrong. In the words of the late and great
Dr Wayne Dyer, "Your life is a parenthesis in eternity, it opens
parenthesis at a given time, called your conception and it closes
parenthesis at a given time, called your death", in between these
two inevitable events is your life, so live it.*

Namaste!

ABOUT THE AUTHOR

Marlon Edward Plaatjies born 07 August 1985, is the last-born son of Charles and Lydia Plaatjies. He is the last of four children birthed to Charles and Lydia. Marlon completed his high-schooling at Eden Park Senior Secondary School in 2003. He is married to his beautiful wife Verlene Plaatjies and is the proud dad of 2 beautiful children, Leyshaen and Matthew.

Since 2004, he started working in various industries and sectors, including the Banking Sector, Call Centres, IT Helpdesk, Sales, Direct Marketing, Insurance and Real Estate to name a few. Over the years he has built extensive experience through the various positions he held and has always been driven and ambitious. This allowed him to soar through the ranks of many of the companies he worked for and to position himself amongst the best within these organizations. In some cases, he was not nearly as qualified as his subordinates but because of his leadership qualities, drive, passion, dedication and commitment, he always found himself in positions of leadership.

In the last few years, Marlon has devoted his life to entrepreneurship and to the GIFTS God bestowed unto him. This, however, came at great personal cost to him, initially, and drove him to a point of severe depression, anxiety, stress and at one point even suicide. Despite all the challenges he faced, he continued to have faith in his dreams of becoming an Author, Speaker, Entrepreneur and Consultant and never gave up on his coveted goal. He is the Co-Founder of The Mevarlion Group along with his brother Averill and sister Cheryl. He is also the Founder and CEO of Marlon E. Plaatjies Global where he lives out his God-given Gift of writing, speaking, creating and innovating. His dedication and passion for helping the needy has sparked in his heart the desire to set up his own charity, The L & M Children's Foundation, named after his two babies, as well as the Mee & Vee Youth Academy that will provide young men and women with essential life and business skills, not taught in schools, to equip them for the world out there.

Marlon is also a Coach and works with South African Households to help them "Get Their Money Right". This program aims to help families who find themselves in financial distress and ruin, to become Financially Free. He also offers Personal Development Coaching to individuals and companies as well as business consulting for SMME's. These programs all focus on improving the individual and the business simultaneously and in so doing, improve the entire organization as a whole.

"My purpose in life is to serve others, this vision for my life was planted into my being back in 2013 during a time of hardship, pain and despair. The work God gave me has to be fulfilled through my various books, audiobooks, seminars and speaking engagements. This is my ministry, my purpose, my calling and I will see to it that I complete this work before I fall asleep." – Marlon E. Plaatjies

God's richest blessings upon you all, may every desire of your heart be made manifest and may you enjoy a life filled with Love, Peace, Laughter, Joy and Prosperity. Blessings to you all.

<hr>

Work with Marlon

If you wish to work with Marlon or to book him for speaking engagements, simply Call, WhatsApp or Email his office on the below contact details:

Email: support@themlmfenix.com
Call or WhatsApp: +27 78 985 6203

SOURCES:

1. https://www.business-humanrights.org/en/latest-news/so-africa-three-million-south-africans-have-lost-their-jobs-as-a-result-of-the-covid-19-pandemic-women-most-affected/

2. https://www.merriam-webster.com/dictionary/principle

3. https://www.etymonline.com/word/principle

4. https://www.iol.co.za/amp/personal-finance/most-south-africans-are-broke-by-the-15th-of-the-month-29270591

5. https://businesstech.co.za/news/finance/440963/this-is-the-average-salary-in-south-africa-right-now-5/amp/

6. http://www.salaryexplorer.com/salary-survey.php?loc=201&loctype=1

7. www.oldmutual.co.za

8. www.easyequities.co.za

9. www.statisticssa.co.za

10. https://image.shutterstock.com-illustration/south-african-rands-isolated-on-260nw-337184099.jpg

11. https://seqlegal.com